# MARKETING BLUNDERS:
## Cases & Lessons For Managers

Zalfa Laili Hamzah & Ong Lin Dar

PARTRIDGE

Copyright © 2020 by Zalfa Laili Hamzah & Ong Lin Dar.

| ISBN: | Softcover | 978-1-5437-6179-5 |
|---|---|---|
|  | eBook | 978-1-5437-6180-1 |

All rights reserved. No part of this book may be used or reproduced by any means, graphic, electronic, or mechanical, including photocopying, recording, taping or by any information storage retrieval system without the written permission of the author except in the case of brief quotations embodied in critical articles and reviews.

Because of the dynamic nature of the Internet, any web addresses or links contained in this book may have changed since publication and may no longer be valid. The views expressed in this work are solely those of the author and do not necessarily reflect the views of the publisher, and the publisher hereby disclaims any responsibility for them.

Print information available on the last page.

**To order additional copies of this book, contact**
Toll Free +65 3165 7531 (Singapore)
Toll Free +60 3 3099 4412 (Malaysia)
orders.singapore@partridgepublishing.com

www.partridgepublishing.com/singapore

# CONTENTS

PREFACE ............................................................................... vii
THE AUTHORS ........................................................................ ix
INTRODUCTION ..................................................................... xi

## PART I
Food and Beverage

CASE STUDY 1: A&W ............................................................... 1
CASE STUDY 2: BURGER KING (RUSSIA) ..................................... 5
CASE STUDY 3: BURGER KING (USA) .......................................... 8
CASE STUDY 4: CADBURY ....................................................... 12
CASE STUDY 5: DOMINO'S PIZZA (RUSSIA) ............................... 16
CASE STUDY 6: DUNKIN' ........................................................ 19
CASE STUDY 7: STARBUCKS .................................................... 23
CASE STUDY 8: SUBWAY ........................................................ 28
CASE STUDY 9: PEPSICO ........................................................ 32
CASE STUDY 10: TROPICANA .................................................. 38

## PART II
Apparel, Beauty Products, and Footwear

CASE STUDY 11: ADIDAS ........................................................ 43
CASE STUDY 12: DOLCE & GABBANA ....................................... 48
CASE STUDY 13: DOVE ........................................................... 51

CASE STUDY 14: GAP...................................................................54
CASE STUDY 15: H&M..................................................................57
CASE STUDY 16: JCPENNEY .......................................................62

**PART III**
Automobile, Banking Services, and Mobile Technology

CASE STUDY 17: BMW...................................................................67
CASE STUDY 18: HSBC ................................................................. 70
CASE STUDY 19: SAMSUNG GALAXY FOLD.............................73
CASE STUDY 20: SAMSUNG GALAXY NOTE 7 ..........................79

KEY TAKEAWAYS ..........................................................................83
CONCLUSION ................................................................................91

# PREFACE

Any mistakes can result in negative consequences and will be interpreted as failure. We often judge others who make mistakes as incompetent and punish them. However, mistakes could be used to illustrate valuable lessons. You can learn a lot from mistakes, either your own or of others. It is the key to success. We learn more from what went wrong than what had been done well.

***Marketing Blunders: Cases and Lessons for Managers*** offers you lessons to learn about some of the most common and typical mistakes cases made by companies. This book presents a collection of a recent case studies in the realms of products, branding and services marketing across different countries and product and services brand categories, including food and beverage, clothing, footwear, personal care, banking services, automotive (cars), and consumer electronics (smartphone and mobile devices). You will learn how to avoid marketing blunders and be able to cope with crisis by learning from the experience of previous crises. The lessons can help you make smart and well-informed decisions when launching marketing campaigns in the future.

This book can be valuable not only to marketers and executives who have the aspiration to succeed in marketing field, but this book will also be useful for postgraduate and undergraduate students who are taking courses related to marketing. After reading the cases, you can make a quick revision by answering discussion questions provided based on the issues. The case study book is believed to be imperative to instructors, researcher and students to better understand the real mistakes and failure in the business world and debate for potential solutions that relevant to current and future business environment.

Let us get started.

# THE AUTHORS

**Dr. Zalfa Laili Hamzah** is a Senior Lecturer at the Graduate School of Business and Department of Marketing, Faculty of Business and Accountancy, University of Malaya, Kuala Lumpur, Malaysia. She has a PhD in Corporate Branding from University of Malaya. Her research interest includes corporate, social media, product and services branding, and consumer behaviour. Her work has been published in the *Journal of Business Research, International Journal of Bank Marketing, Journal of Consumer Marketing, Management Review Quarterly,* and *International Journal of Internet Marketing and Advertising.* Dr. Zalfa has taught several marketing courses for postgraduate and undergraduate students, including Global Branding, Brand Management, Strategic Marketing, Marketing Management, Consumer Behaviour, Integrated Marketing Communication, Services Marketing, and Retailing.

**Dr. Ong Lin Dar** is a Senior Lecturer in the Department of Business Strategy and Policy at University of Malaya, Kuala Lumpur, Malaysia. She completed her PhD at University of Malaya in 2012. She was awarded a Certificate of Excellent Service, University of Malaya in 2016. Her field of interests includes business management, organisational behaviour, leadership, business communication, and human resource management. Her work has appeared in a range of journals, including the *International Journal of Occupational Safety and Ergonomics,* and the *South African Journal of Business Management.*

# INTRODUCTION

'Marketing is all, and everything is marketing'. It is not just a business function; it is a way of doing business. It is everybody's job in the organisation. All companies recognise the benefits of marketing in their quest to survive and prosper in an increasingly competitive business world. It is an essential part of having a successful business. If done right, you can attract new customers and keep your current customers. If things go wrong, it will definitely cost companies more than just loss of sales and loyal customers. You also have to deal with disgruntled customers, angry posts on social media, bad press, and so on.

Marketing is all about customers, and it is not easy to win their hearts and minds. Marketing blunders can happen to any company. However, mistakes are not failures. They teach us about what 'did' and 'did not' work. Learn from them, and do not repeat the same mistakes. Mark Zuckerberg believes, 'Don't even bother avoiding making mistakes because you're going to make tonnes of mistakes and the important thing is to learn quickly from the mistakes you make and to not give up'.

Success sometimes leads to trouble. Well-established companies thought they could do anything and make any changes they like in the marketplace. They changed their product design, logo, packaging, or pricing schemes without any explicit communication with customers prior to the changes. They launched advertising campaigns that are offensive to their target audience, without clear objectives, full of stereotypes, and so on. These mistakes were extremely costly for companies, both to their budgets and their reputations.

When customers had unfavourable brand experience, they may become annoyed. Some of them take actions to complain or even boycott. Therefore, crafting a well-thought-out marketing strategy is necessary for all companies.

To keep your business on the road to success, it is always a good idea to

1. ***Know yourself.*** Understand your business strengths and weaknesses. Identify your competitive advantage and find ways to capitalise on that advantage. Consider your marketing experiences and learn from past encounters.
2. ***Know your customers.*** Take some time to investigate your customers and the market. Perform a comprehensive brand audit to examine what they think and feel about your brand. Furthermore, use a variety of technology-based communications to create and sustain goodwill with your customers. Good communication is worth every minute it takes and every cent it costs.
3. ***Know your competitors.*** Make a list of your current and future competitors. Do a SWOT (strengths, weaknesses, opportunities, and threats) analysis on them. Learn from their failures and successes, and set yourself apart from the

competition. Sun Tzu said in *The Art of War*, 'Know the enemy and know yourself; in a hundred battles you will never be in peril. When you are ignorant of the enemy but know yourself, your chances of winning or losing are equal. If ignorant both of your enemy and yourself, you are certain in every battle to be in peril'. Make competition work for you. Sometimes collaborating with a competitor is actually the best way to achieve a common business goal and grow your company.

Start doing your research now if you want to avoid any marketing blunders of all time. Learn what they are and how to avoid them.

# PART I
# FOOD AND BEVERAGE

A&W
Burger King (Russia)
Burger King (USA)
Cadbury
Domino's Pizza (Russia)
Dunkin'
Starbucks
Subway
PepsiCo
Tropicana

# CASE STUDY 1: A&W

## MENU NAMES CHANGED

A&W Restaurants is well-known for its root beer float, burgers, waffles, and coney. The company was founded in 1919 by Roy W. Allen, who set up a roadside stand. The name A&W came from the initials of Roy W. Allen and Frank Wright, his partner who joined him in 1922 to open their first restaurant. A&W franchised its first outlet in 1924. The chains serve great-tasting burgers, onion rings, and A&W Root Beer in frosted mugs. A&W is always looking for ways to strengthen its unique brand image and identity to differentiate its brand from competitors. One of the ways was to introduce its mascot, The Great Root Bear, also called Rooty. The mascot is featured in various A&W's community events and exhibitions to engage with its customers and boost its online presence. Using Rooty as the mascot is a great way for A&W to bring people together and create lasting memories with the brand in the consumers' minds. More importantly, the mascot is used to build a strong connection with the target market, improve brand visibility, strengthen its brand identity, and increase brand recall and recognition.

A&W began expanding its business worldwide by opening its first Canadian restaurant in Winnipeg, Manitoba, in 1956. In 1963, A&W was extended to the Philippines, Japan, and Malaysia. There are approximately one thousand A&W Restaurants worldwide in 2019. A&W reached Malaysia in 1963, and its first store was located in Jalan Tuanku Abdul Rahman, followed by the first drive-in restaurant in Petaling Jaya in 1965. A&W had aggressively expanded the reach of its business in 2008. However, twenty-seven A&W outlets were closed since 2011, while other outlets needed to reposition their business and operations to achieve sustainable growth. The closure of the outlets as part of business operation relocation and company's recovering efforts of costs losing.

A&W has heavily applied traditional marketing channels in promoting its brand compared to digital marketing, website, and social media. Due to that, A&W has yet to maximise its reach to a larger audience. Aside from that, the prices of A&W were slightly higher than their competitors. One of the marketing issues experienced by A&W Malaysia was the food names on the menu, such as 'Coney Dog' and 'Root Beer'. In 2013, the name 'Coney Dog' was changed to 'Beef Coney' or 'Chicken Coney', while the name 'Root Beer' was changed to 'RB'. The names had to be changed to avoid confusion among Muslim consumers. Malaysian authorities will not issue halal certification for non-alcoholic 'beer' or any products using haram words like 'dog', 'ham', or 'bacon'. This includes the use of the term 'halal beer' in contravention of the manual procedure for Malaysia Halal Certification, even though it does not contain non-halal ingredients.

The Malaysian Islamic Development Department, a government religious authority that produces and certify halal label, told A&W

to remove the word 'dog' from its menu to secure itself the halal status. Although its products do not contain dog meat, the dog is considered unclean in Islam, and the name cannot be related to halal certification. *Halal* means 'permissible' in Arabic. Pork and its by-products, alcohol, and animals not slaughtered in accordance with Islamic procedures are all *haram* or prohibited. Following the standard halal requirement, A&W also renamed its canned or bottled ginger beer and root beer produced by local manufacturers to Ginger Ade and Sarsaparilla, respectively.

**Lessons from A&W:**

- *Be creative and unique in the differentiation of the brand name.* It is ideal to use a mascot as a marketing tool. Consumers can remember and recognise A&W easily because of its unique Great Root Bear mascot.
- *Be clear about the crafted meaning of values or messages.* Every company must communicate its values or messages clearly to the consumers. Make sure you deliver the right information and your message is consistent across all channels. Use multiple channels to reach wider customers including both young and old generations. Utilise the advantage of social media and digital marketing platforms extensively to increase high visibility and awareness.
- *Be humble when communicating with your customers.* Companies have to set aside their ego, drop their prejudice, and learn how to communicate clearly and consistently to the market be it local or international. Be able to create differentiation among competitors.
- *Be professional and respectful of other cultures.* Marketing executives need to recognise the importance of diversity

in advertising and how to integrate brand and culture successfully. Hire experts in your target countries to understand cultural sensitivity especially language meaning, symbols, colours and rules of religion.

- *Be sure to choose appropriate names for your products*. A good name is the best insurance for long-term success. It is critical as it may affect the perception of the customers. Notably, all companies need to consider the meaning of the brand name and be aware of its relations to cultural and religion issues. The right name should be simple, catchy, relatively short, and easy to spell. Get feedback on the name and make sure that it does not have any negative connotations.

## Discussion Questions:

1. What are the cultural environments or variables that could affect marketers in the development of advertising and promotion programmes in a foreign market?
2. Explain how cultural variables have created problems for a company in the development of advertising, promotion, and branding strategies.
3. Discuss the meaning of 'think globally, act locally', 'global products, local messages', with regard to advertising design and its brand elements.
4. What do you understand about halal logo and halal marketing?
5. Suggest how A&W will be able to promote and advertise their brand more effectively in the future.

# CASE STUDY 2: BURGER KING (RUSSIA)

## A SEXIST ADVERTISEMENT

James McLamore and David Edgerton acquired Insta-Burger King in 1954. They renamed the restaurant to Burger King. The Miami-based fast-food chain has now ballooned to more than 10,000 restaurants globally. The company opened its first outlet in Russia in January 2010 and now has more than 550 outlets in the country.

Russia hosted the FIFA World Cup for the first time in 2018. To celebrate the World Cup, Burger King Russia offered three million rubles (US$47,000) and a free lifetime supply of Whoppers to Russian women who get impregnated by a Russian national team player. The advertisement was posted in a social media post with a woman holding her baby bump. Burger King Russia claimed that the reward was made to ensure the continued success of Russia national football team in the future. The post ended with a call: 'Go ahead! We believe in you!'

The post was clearly offensive. Critics assailed the offer as sexist and demeaning. The advertisement was quickly pulled off following backlash from the public. Burger King Russia immediately issued an apology for the advertisement. They admitted the campaign turned out to be 'too insulting'.

Likewise, Burger King's American headquarters apologised for the advertisement in a press statement and stated the offer did not represent the company's values. It added, 'We are taking steps to ensure this type of activity does not happen again'.

**Lessons from Burger King (Russia):**

- *Beware of what you intend to post on social media.* Make sure the campaigns do not contain sexist, demeaning, and sensitive content, no matter who your target audience is.
- *Fix the problem before it is too late.* Keep an eye on your social media account and quickly react if you discover any negative reviews.
- *Apologise if you have made mistakes.* It is crucial for you to admit a mistake and say sorry for making a distasteful advertising campaign.
- *Try to clean up a public relations mess.* Show your sincerity in fixing the problems by making public apology.
- *Learn from past mistakes.* Make sure you do not make any similar mistakes in the future.

**Discussion Questions:**

1. Burger King thought it was a great idea to offer cash rewards and free Whoppers to Russian women who managed to get impregnated by players competing in the World Cup. Do you think Burger King's Russia division was joking about the advertisement? Do you think Russian women will take up the offer? Discuss.
2. How can global companies like Burger King ensure that this type of offensive campaign does not happen again?
3. Why many marketing campaigns are still sexist and misrepresent women? Does it pay to use sexual and humour appeals in advertising?

# CASE STUDY 3: BURGER KING (USA)

## AVOID BRAND VALUES CONFUSION

Burger King is a multinational American chain of fast-food restaurants serving hamburgers. The company was founded in 1953 as Insta-Burger King, a restaurant chain based in Jacksonville, Florida. After Insta-Burger King ran into financial difficulties in 1954, its two Miami-based franchisees, David Edgerton and James McLamore, purchased the company and renamed it Burger King. Burger King's menu had been expanded from the primary offering of burgers, French fries, sodas, and milkshakes to a broader and more diverse range of products. In 1957, the Whopper became the first significant addition to the menu. It had since become the signature product of Burger King.

Burger King has introduced many products worldwide. However, some of its products have failed in the United States. In April 2019, Burger King launched the meat-free Impossible Whopper in 59 restaurants in the St. Louis area, followed by the opening of 7,200 U.S. locations. Burger King advertised vegetarian patty, topped with tomatoes, lettuce, pickles, onions, ketchup, and mayonnaise, as '100% Whopper, 0% Beef'.

In November 2019, Mr. Phillip Williams, who practices a strict vegan diet, filed a lawsuit against Burger King in Florida. The class-action suit accused Burger King of undertaking false and misleading business practices in advertising its plant-based burgers. He bought the Impossible Whopper via the drive-through in Atlanta store and claimed that there was no signage at the drive-through indicating that the meat-free burger would be cooked on the same grills as beef or chicken products. He asked for compensation and urged Burger King to stop cooking the Impossible Whoppers on standard grills.

A representative for Burger King said customers could ask their Impossible Whopper patties to be prepared in the oven. However, the consumers claimed that they were unaware of such an option. This revealed that there was a misunderstanding about the clarity of the process in preparing Impossible Whopper.

As a result, Burger King filed a motion to dismiss the allegation that the fast-food chain tricked their customers into thinking that their Impossible Whopper was completely vegan, even it was cooked on the same grill as other meat products. Burger King never labelled the product as a vegan in its advertising. Burger King then requested the judge to dismiss the allegation that the plant-based Impossible Whopper had been misrepresented in March 2020. Furthermore, Impossible Foods Inc. explained that Impossible Whopper was a product for meat-eaters who wanted to consume less animal protein. Still, it was not for vegans or vegetarians. This statement was posted on its website that described the Impossible Burger as 100% Whopper,

0% Beef and added that for guests looking for a meat-free option, a non-broiler method of preparation is available upon request.

After investigation, a report confirmed that the Florida Judge had dismissed the lawsuit against Burger King. The plaintiffs were unable to provide sufficient evidence and did not enquire about the cooking method. Besides, there was no promise in Burger King's advertisement that vegetable patties would be prepared on a different surface.

**Lessons from Burger King (USA):**

- *Deliver great service and experience to customers.* Engage with customers in radical empathy and make it your goal to delight customers. All companies should always show that they care about customers and are willing to listen. Regularly get feedback from customers to know if the company correctly interprets the value of the brand and always sends the right message to them.
- *Respond immediately to failure.* Any marketing mistakes can be an opportunity to strengthen customer relationships and become better. If the problem is not well handled, some consumers may punish the company because they have experienced a sense of betrayal and injustice. When a company received complaints, it must quickly investigate the problems and follow through with action to fix it.
- *Communicate messages consistently with brand values.* Any product or service failure can spread very fast and lead to customer backlash. Negligence occurs when the service has not been performed as promised, and the customers' expectations have not been met. All companies need to

rethink their brand strategy to ensure that they deliver on brand promises.

**Discussion Questions:**

1. Identify the mistakes made by Burger King in this case. What led to those mistakes?
2. If you are a consultant, what would you suggest to Burger King's management to solve the problems more effectively?
3. Critically assess the effectiveness of the current practices of Burger King in handling complaints and the lawsuits. What did they do well, and what did they do not do well? Do you think their recovery strategies have worked well? Why?
4. How can Burger King utilise the Internet, its websites, and social media sites to manage its customers' perception and brand experience?

# CASE STUDY 4: CADBURY

## CONTROVERSIAL ADVERTISING CAMPAIGN

Cadbury, formerly Cadbury's and Cadbury Schweppes, is known for its iconic chocolate bar, Dairy Milk chocolate. It is a multinational British confectionery company. Since 2010, Cadbury has been wholly owned by Mondelez International, headquartered in Uxbridge, West London, and operates in more than fifty countries around the world. In 1824, John Cadbury began selling tea, coffee, and chocolate from his premises in Birmingham. Cadbury established a business with his brother Benjamin and later his sons Richard and George. George developed the Bournville estate, a model village designed to improve the living conditions of the company employees. Dairy Milk chocolate was introduced in 1905. It consumed a higher proportion of milk in the recipe compared with competing products. By 1914, chocolate was the company's best-selling product.

Cadbury chocolate company introduced a new logo for the first time in fifty years in April 2020. The company spent £1 million to modify the logo. The logo was based on the signature of William Cadbury, the grandson of John, who set the firm path back in the 1820s. The new logo 'puts the humanity back' into the design, with the lighter lines replacing the thick lettering in the previous version, which focused on tilted writing. The new elevated packaging included a redrawn wordmark, unique iconography, and typography, making the look appeared more natural, authentic, and of high quality. Nevertheless, there were some criticisms on the new logo. Some people claimed that they cannot spot the difference, and it was a waste of money.

However, this is not the first time that Cadbury has courted controversy. In March 2019, Birmingham chocolate giant Cadbury launched a Freddo Treasures advertising campaign with the theme of a real treasure hunt on its websites. The pieces were 'grab a metal detector', 'go hunting for Roman riches', and 'dig holes looking for gold or treasure'. The new website for treasure hunting comprised sites across the United Kingdom and Ireland, namely a fair game of treasure that encouraged children to hunt for real Romans. The advertisement campaign was meant to inspire families 'to go on everyday adventures together'. However, this campaign provoked a backlash from the archaeologists and social media.

Archaeologists have labelled the campaign as 'intensely stupid' and 'irresponsible'. The campaign suggested that all treasure-hunting is okay and advocated youngsters to dig protected landscapes without permission. Moreover, Cadbury did not issue any reminders that unauthorised mining is illegal and people could be prosecuted for doing so. However, Cadbury refuted the allegation and claimed that the company had no intention to encourage people to break the law. The company had taken down the advertising campaign webpage and updated the webpage content to focus on directing families to museums.

**Lessons from Cadbury:**

- *Be clear about the objectives of the advertisement campaigns.* A company needs to know its audience and what it wants to accomplish from the outset of marketing campaigns. Ensure that message is clear and hits your target. Always keep up with audience changes and tweak your advertising accordingly. Carefully craft marketing campaigns and plan out well in advance.
- *Respect cultural, legal, and heritage issues.* Cultural heritage means a shared bond, our belonging to a community that represents our history and our identity, our bond to the past, to our present, and the future. Culture should, therefore, be conserved and preserved for future generations. Companies should be cautious at all times by meeting all legal, ethical, and moral requirements.
- *Be careful with your message.* Take some time to learn more about customers and fine-tune your marketing efforts to optimise your marketing budget. Also, send the right message to the right person at the right time. If you make a mistake, own it, make it right, and move on.

**Discussion Questions:**

1. Archaeologists claimed that Cadbury's advertising campaign encouraged children to dig up treasure at important sites across the United Kingdom. Do you think the campaign will encourage illegal excavation and looting? Discuss.
2. Based on your understanding, do you believe that customers correctly interpret the values communicated through this campaign?
3. Suggest how Cadbury could design better advertising campaigns in the future.

# CASE STUDY 5: DOMINO'S PIZZA (RUSSIA)

## AN OVERPROMISED CAMPAIGN

American pizza giant Domino's Pizza is the largest pizza-delivery operator in the world. Founded in 1960, the pizza firm has more than seventeen thousand locations in over ninety markets around the world. One of its important distinctive features is its strong and bright logo. The three dots in the logo served as a symbol of the first three restaurants the franchise opened.

In 1998, Domino's Pizza opened its first restaurant in Russia. Currently, there are around 180 Domino's Pizza in the country. In September 2018, the independent franchise owner in Russia launched a 'Domino's Forever' campaign on social media. The pizza chain offered up to one hundred free pizzas each year for one hundred years to customers that got tattoos of the company's logo on any visible parts of their body. The customers were asked to share the photograph on social media with a hashtag (#Dominance, in Russian word). Once a picture was posted, the participants would receive an authentication gift certificate from Domino's Pizza Russia.

The campaign began on 31 August 2018 and was originally planned to run for two months. However, it went viral, and there were so many people who got the tattoos in exchange for a lifelong supply of pizza. In merely five days, more than 300 people took up the offer. Unfortunately, the chain did not expect the campaign to have such a huge turnout for the event. It then had to cap the number of eligible participants to 350 for the special lifetime deal. It also stipulated that the tattoo must be at least 2 cm in length.

The company announced an urgent update of submission closure on its social media account on 4 September 2018. In the end, there were 381 people who took part in the campaign. Domino's Pizza Russia clearly underestimated the number of people willing to get a small tattoo in exchange for up to ten thousand pizzas.

**Lessons from Domino's Pizza (Russia):**

- *Get your customers to be your ambassadors.* Your customers can serve as your walking billboards. Virtually any space, including human bodies, is a potential medium for a marketer's advertisement.
- *Evaluate campaign response.* Do not underestimate on what length your customers would go to get a deal or offer you made. Be careful and do not overpromise in your promotional campaign.
- *Manage your promises.* Set realistic expectations about your campaign offer and cap a limit on it if you cannot be sure to deliver it unconditionally.
- *Control the ramifications of out-of-control campaign.* Call off the promotion immediately if it went out of hand to prevent further losses.

**Discussion Questions:**

1. In September 2018, Domino's Pizza used the human bodies as its advertisement medium in Russia. More than three hundred people were tattooed with the brand's logo for the exchange of free pizza. In your opinion, is tattoo advertising effective or ineffective? Explain.
2. Domino's Pizza Russia team had to abruptly cancel its Domino's Forever campaign just days after it was launched on social media. Why? How did customers react after Domino's Pizza called off the promotion?
3. What are other alternative advertising mediums Domino's Pizza can use to increase its brand loyalty?

# CASE STUDY 6: DUNKIN'

## MISALIGNMENT BRAND POSITIONING

Dunkin', formerly known as Dunkin Donuts, is a multinational American coffee and doughnut shop. It was founded by William Rosenberg in Quincy, Massachusetts, in 1950. Dunkin' is one of the world's leading franchises of Quick Service Restaurants (QSRs) serving hot and cold coffee and baked goods, with almost thirteen thousand restaurants in 46 countries worldwide.

In September 2019, the 'Donuts' in the coffee chain was dropped from its brand name in a rebranding exercise to become Dunkin'. The rebranding undertook the transformation of innovative elements, including visual identity, name, new store design, digital-order kiosks, packaging, and drinks, such as nitro-infused cold brewing. The rebranding was intended for growth to modernise Dunkin's experience by having a brighter, lighter feel with nostalgic touches, such as bringing forward the bakery case and more modern amenities that met the needs and demands of today's on-the-go customers. Dunkin's primary technique was to offer breakfast to the morning market. This was a strategy that operated effectively in the United States. It was one that the organisation employed when it continued to operate and expand in other countries. However, when it was marketed globally, local cultures also affected the flavours and preferences of the food menu.

Despite the worldwide expansion of the market, Dunkin' continued to struggle in the Indian market. In 2012, Dunkin' merged with Jubilant Foodworks Limited, launched the first Dunkin' in India, and eventually expanded to seventy-seven stores across the country. Dunkin' granted exclusive franchise privileges to Jubilant Foodworks and decided to add core Dunkin' goods, along with more localised menu items, to appeal to local tastes. As Dunkin' tried to get the recipe right in India, it concentrated on things like burgers that had strayed away from the doughnuts and coffee for which it had long been popular. Besides, Dunkin' delivered a more personalised, tailored, and more variety menu than its US outlets, revamping its restaurant experience to cater to the taste buds of young Indian shoppers and the middle-class households and to satisfy the needs of the American office-goers who typically had breakfast on-the-go.

However, the company closed thirty-seven stores by the end of June 2018, which was more than half of its unprofitable outlets in India to reduce operating and overhead costs. The corporation had struggled to make any substantial money. As a result, Dunkin' refocused its main offerings, and Jubilant continued to optimise the store accounts and prices.

Any of the factors identified were attributable to the company's loss. India was a great nation with a variety of languages and traditions, with every area changing its cuisine. As such, their eating style would not be comparable to Western society, which favoured on-the-go breakfast.

In addition, many Indians were involved in having a family breakfast at home every day. They perceived doughnuts as a snack rather than a breakfast menu. In reality, their local sweet food was not the same as Dunkin's sweet taste. The central offering of Dunkin' Donuts doughnuts and coffee was not following the Indian breakfast model, as the Indians were not familiar with the idea of providing doughnuts for breakfast.

Third, local vendors (known as *mithaiwalas*, who offered sweet snacks) also had a deeper connection, cultural similarities, and a good relationship with local buyers. This contributed to low demand for the doughnuts. This situation portrayed why Dunkin' Donuts struggled to seize India's daily breakfast.

**Lessons from Dunkin':**

- *Think globally and act locally.* In strategizing product positioning, being relevant to local consumers is the key to the global success of a product. Global brands must adapt their businesses to local markets to succeed.
- *Understand the needs and wants of the target consumers.* It is essential to drive sales and ensure business sustainability. Do lots of research before expanding into international markets. Always be flexible and be willing to change.
- *Be sensitive to different cultures.* Different markets favour different marketing and sales approaches. Target the right international markets and adapt your products and strategies to appeal to local customers. Think differently, embrace cultural sensitivity, and hold a customer-first attitude.

**Discussion Questions:**

1. Why do you think that Dunkin' had decided to expand internationally?
2. Explain how Dunkin's marketing mix will adapt to Indian markets.
3. Identify the mistakes of Dunkin'. What kind of advice would you give to Dunkin' to avoid these mistakes in the future?
4. Do you think that Dunkin' should allow local operators to make their own decisions about the flavours of ice creams, doughnuts, and other items to be sold in the country? How would you recommend that the global management of the company assess the cultural differences in each market?

# CASE STUDY 7: STARBUCKS

## OUTLET LOCATION MATTERS

The Starbucks Company, headquartered in Seattle, Washington, is a multinational American coffeehouse and roasting chain. The company was founded in Seattle's Pike Place Market in 1971 by Jerry Baldwin, Zev Siegl, and Gordon Bowker. The company's mission statement is 'to inspire and nurture the human spirit— one person, one cup, and one neighbourhood at a time'. This mission reflects the value of building a community of happy and satisfied customers one step at a time. Starbucks is seen as the most massive manifestation of the second generation of coffee culture in the United States as the world's biggest coffeehouse chain. Starbucks operates more than thirty thousand sites worldwide in more than seventy countries as of the beginning of 2020.

Starbucks stores deliver hot and cold drinks, whole-bean coffee, micro-ground instant coffee known as VIA, espresso, caffe latte, complete- and loose-leaf teas like Teavana tea brands, Evolution New juices, Frappuccino beverages, La Boulange pastries, and snacks, such as chips and crackers; some offerings are seasonal or specific to the locality of the store.

Despite offerings and well-positioned brands, Starbucks revealed in 2019 that low sales had led to the closure of 150 stores in the United States. However, the same store revenue is expected to rise by only 1 per cent this year, which would be the worst since 2009. Among the factors identified for the closure of the stores are excessive locations, overpricing, plenty of rivalries, application of technology, and retail issues. Starbucks faces market saturation because of an abundance of stores located in a big city. This leads to a major problem with the cannibalisation of stores, where one store loses sales as a result of other new stores, making customers less loyal to one store.

Furthermore, the company raised its beverage prices, which caused fewer transactions and a slowdown in sales. The rise in prices was because of rising labour and non-coffee commodity costs. Starbucks applies price hikes to separate themselves from the pack and reinforce the premium image of their brand. This value was communicated through ad campaigns to manipulate customer perception.

Besides, Starbucks confronts heavy competition in the beverage business, particularly with significant competitors, such as Dunkin' and McDonald's. These large competitors entice some of the customers to offer more attractive drinks from these coffee concepts. Starbucks has also entered the coffee beans and ground coffee market by distributing its product line to retailers and grocery stores around the world as part of the process of expanding its retail segment. Other than direct competitors, Starbucks has two indirect competitors from the dry coffee goods market, namely Maxwell House and Folgers. Maxwell House is one of the top-performing subsidiaries of Kraft

Corporation, and Folgers is the largest selling ground coffee in the United States.

In addition, the decline in customers' patronage of shopping mall traffic is also attributed to a traffic reduction in Starbucks stores. This is because the pattern of consumer spending has changed, they spend more time at home, and more of them brew their artisanal coffee and consume more ready-to-drink coffee and other beverages. The growth in online and mobile ordering also lead to a drop in sales and customer loyalty.

**Lessons from Starbucks:**

- *Be smart in choosing a strategic business location.* The first thing the company should bear in mind is *location, location, location!* Think about customer needs, expectations, and the nature of the services when deciding the location of the stores.
- *Be a standout and avoid having the same business outlet in the same area.* Suppose you want to open another store of the same type, distance your store to avoid store cannibalisation. When this happens, sales of existing stores will drop because some customers begin to shop in a nearby store, particularly for franchise business models. If a new territory is established too close to an existing store, relations with other franchisees may be damaged. As a result, one of the stores may not be able to increase sales well.
- *Be innovative to enhance the loyalty programme.* Take care of loyal customers. It is essential to find ways to retain existing customers. Renew or redesign loyalty programmes to provide customers with more redemptions and payment options. Find an appropriate approach to keep existing customers.

Remember, maintaining existing customers is cheaper than acquiring new ones. This is because the cost of acquiring a new customer can be up to seven times higher.

- ***Be sensitive to consumer trend and preference changes.*** Customer needs and desires are dynamic. The company must be able to act more quickly to meet the ever-changing tastes and conditions of the customers. The company should be creative in positioning its brand to ensure that it continues to gain its competitive advantage and increase the agility of innovation. Having core value drivers could serve as a foundation for accelerating growth and creating long-term shareholder value.

- ***Be sensitive to price change.*** A company should always show that it cares for its customers and knows what they need. Always be realistic and ethical in making decisions about pricing for financial solvency and consider the pros and cons of price setting. Understanding the level of customer income is central. Customers are divided into either sensitive or insensitive to the price changes. Companies must have a good understanding of the costs, the new values created, and the pricing of competitors.

- ***Be effective at communicating price changes and consumer benefits.*** Customers find the price and benefit/value balance that would best satisfy their needs. Starbucks understands that most of its customer base is relatively price-insensitive and uses small price increases that are barely noticeable by everyday consumers to boost margins. Quantify your buyer personas, and the demand for your product or service will help you choose a price that captures the maximum amount that your customers are willing to pay. Whenever a change is made, ensure that the brand attributes offered are effectively communicated to the target market. Customers should be better informed about price changes with good value offerings. Notably, the company must be careful in setting a new price to avoid confusing customers, accusations of unethical behaviour, loss of trust, and customer dissatisfaction.

**Discussion Questions:**

1. What are the factors that accounted for the success of Starbucks in the early day of business? What are the value propositions of Starbucks?
2. Why did Starbucks' sales decline? Provide suggestions to management on how to improve sales in the future by addressing the factors identified in the above case that led to a decline in sales.
3. Identify major pricing strategies and discuss the importance of understanding customer-value perceptions and competing strategies when setting prices.
4. Discuss the internal and external factors that may have an impact on the pricing decisions of the product.

# CASE STUDY 8: SUBWAY

## UNDELIVERED BRAND PROMISE: 'EAT FRESH'

Subway was a small privately-opened American restaurant franchise, which mainly sold submarine sandwiches (subs) and salads in 1965. The company was founded by Dr. Peter Buck, a nuclear physicist, who changed the life of Fred DeLuca, a college student, to open a submarine sandwich store to help pay for his tuition fees. Dr. Peter made an initial investment of $1,000, and the store was renamed Subway in 1968, becoming the second-largest fast-food advertiser in the United States, behind only McDonald's.

As of July 2020, Subway has approximately more than forty-one thousand locations in more than one hundred countries around the world. Subway implemented the advertising slogan 'Eat Fresh'. It focused on how its sandwiches were made from freshly-baked bread and fresh ingredients, in front of customers to their exact specifications, by employees whom Subway called Subway Sandwich Artists.

Subway's vision statement is to 'be the #1 Quick Service Restaurant (QSR) franchise in the world while delivering fresh, delicious sandwiches and an exceptional experience'. Subway aims to ensure that the business only serves the best dishes and superior food experience. The core brand values of Subway are to have the best quality menu offerings that everyone in any part of the world can afford and enjoy. Moreover, by offering nutritious food ingredients, Subway promises to build a better relationship with customers. As such, the brand has committed itself to make the most delicate sandwiches and meals with the most efficient, safest, and best-tasting items. In reality, Subway has established and maintained rigorous internal food protection systems and procedures that comply with food safety and quality standards for food safety management in restaurants. Because of this rarity, the fast-food sandwich industry was dominated by Subway.

Despite these value-added deals, it was reported in 2017 that more than nine hundred U.S. stores in the Subway sandwich chain were shut down because of reduced and not lucrative national revenues. Following the news, significant consumer owners, franchisees, and employees expressed their views to share their discontent with the consistency and freshness of Subway's food. Customers were initially entirely impressed by the promise of 'Eat Fresh' brand values, which was the freshness of their ingredients and the delight of their subs, also by the idea that a 'sandwich artist' would do it right in front of the customer and add whatever the customer asked the 'sandwich artist' to do.

In 2017, some consumers claimed that Subway has failed to keep up with their demands for local and fresh ingredients. A possible explanation of this undelivered brand promise is that franchisees and employees claimed that most Subway locations could receive only one or two shipments of fresh produce per week. Because of that, a lot of the lettuce obtained was sometimes near expiry. Not only that, the vacuum packed can still brown and often contributing to soggy and spoiled vegetables. Subway responded that it worked with more than one hundred family farms and suppliers in the United States to help ensure that fresh produce was available in its restaurants. From farm to the sandwich, they had a strict food quality standard, which guaranteed the freshest products. Franchisees are given freedom when they want to schedule lettuce delivery either once a week or twice a week. Therefore, suppliers should decide when their orders should be scheduled to ensure that they always had fresh produce in the restaurant. Despite Subway's claims, franchisees and employees were still not satisfied with Subway's policy of less freedom to schedule lettuce delivery.

Regardless of the argument between Subway and the suppliers, Subway needs to resolve and gain back customer trust. Customers never care about the internal problems of management; they only demand Subway fulfil its brand promise of 'Eat Fresh'. Subway then should get back in touch with their roots by delivering freshly baked bread and fresh ingredients assembled with care.

**Lessons from Subway:**

- ***Be ethical and honest in delivering brand values*** as brand values build customer trust and perception. Brands are more than just names and symbols. Whatever the company offers, as on the label or tagline, is considered to be a promise and should be consistently delivered. The unfulfilled promise of the brand will spoil the brand image and lead to a bad brand reputation.

- *Never break the brand promise.* It will damage brand trust and brand reputation. A brand represents consumer's perceptions and feelings about product performance. Customers are smarter and more knowledgeable about nutrition and food sourcing nowadays.
- *Build strong franchisor-franchisee relationships.* Franchisors should outline clear expectations from the start and maintain consistent communications with their franchisees. By actively obtaining the information about what franchisees want and need, franchisors can provide the necessary support and resources to their franchisees.
- *Keep up with competition.* Competition exists in every field. Understanding your unique selling points and what your competitors are doing can help your business grow. Learn relevant competitors' strategy too for business to remain competitive.

**Discussion Questions:**

1. How does Subway position its brand?
2. Do you think that Subway has broken its brand promise? Discuss.
3. Give suggestions on how Subway can improve its brand image and customer perception.
4. How do you perceive the relationships between Subway management and its suppliers as well as customers? Suggest how to improve those relationships.

# CASE STUDY 9: PEPSICO

## THE PEPSI BRAND MISSTEP

PepsiCo, Inc. is a multinational American food, snack, and beverage corporation founded in 1965. Pepsi is one of the leading soda beverages brands in the industry involved in the manufacturing, marketing, and distribution of grain-based snack foods, beverages, and other products.

PepsiCo is the second-largest food and beverage business in the world. PepsiCo's vision is to be the global leader in convenient foods and beverages by winning with purpose. This vision manifests its goal of sustainably winning the marketplace and all aspects of the business and giving customers more choices. In 2019, PepsiCo generated more than $67 billion in net revenue from more than two hundred countries and territories worldwide. Revenues were generated from a wide range of complimentary food and beverage portfolios, including Frito-Lay, Gatorade, Pepsi-Cola, Quaker, and Tropicana. The company consists of PepsiCo Beverages North America, Frito-Lay North America, Quaker Foods North America;

Latin America; Europe; Africa, Middle East, and South Asia; and the Asia Pacific, Australia, New Zealand, and China.

The soda beverage industry is characterised by intense competition. PepsiCo invests extensively in marketing as it is a crucial factor for business growth, particularly in advertising and promotion, as well as in product innovation. Pepsi has been famous for producing exciting marketing campaigns. It has positioned itself as a brand of snack and beverage that includes nutritious and low-calorie choices other than regular soda products. There are twenty-two iconic billion-dollar brands in its portfolio. Pepsi has invested $2.4 billion solely in advertising. However, with the advent of new media, particularly with the rise of digital technology, marketing promotional activities have shifted. Most of Pepsi's advertising budget goes to digital media and ads. With the advent of social media, PepsiCo interacts with its consumers in real-time with advertising campaigns.

Pepsi has positioned its brand reflecting youthful energy, and this is often a significant trend across its advertising and marketing campaigns. Its brand focuses on millennials, including teenagers and youths with a modern and fast-moving lifestyle. Pepsi has maintained an affordable pricing strategy that caters to all segments of income, from the lower-middle class to the upper class. In 2017, PepsiCo launched a campaign called 'Live for Now – Moments'. It also commenced an existing 'Live for Now' campaign created by the company in 2012. This campaign received a high level of criticism, incorporating the ad 'Jump in Pepsi Moments' to reach millennials and 'to project a global message of unity, peace, and understanding'.

PepsiCo's marketing team explained that the craft of 'jump in' the ad by putting all people in a rally was perceived as beautiful and socially responsible to show that they agreed and able to make everyone join and buy Pepsi. The advertisement featured a staged protest full of hired actors, including twenty-one-year-old supermodel Kendall Jenner. Many people criticised the ad for its insensitive approach. Some viewers discovered improper execution of the desired message. The scene started with Jenner, in a blond wig and a silver dress, posing like a supermodel. At the same time, crowds of millennials walked on the streets while holding placards. In contrast, the musician had decided to join and sign Kendall to join the protest. Finally, Jenner decided to join the protest by removing her wig, changing clothes, and wiping her makeup. In the ad, Jenner joined the protest and eventually approached the cop, who was standing guard over the protestors, with a can of Pepsi and then took a sip. The protesters were very excited about the actions of the police and Kendall.

Kendall Jenner was a fashion model, a reality star. She was acting as a brand ambassador for Estée Lauder's multimedia ad campaign. Jenner appeared on the cover of Love and Victoria's Secret and grew up with the Kardashian's family show. There were arguments about Jenner's ability as a spokesperson for PepsiCo as she was not a relevant person to their message and corporate social responsibility for the core-specific campaign. She was not known for activism or speaking out on any social issues.

A controversy began two days after the campaign was released. As a consequence, there was much condemnation of PepsiCo's social media campaign. For instance, Twitter users expressed concern and disgust at the ad's release, claiming that it trivialised real-life protests in which several people lost their lives fighting for a real cause. Besides, some users remarked that protesters would not get tear-gassed if the cops handed a Pepsi to the cops.

Many other tweets were so angry with Jenner that the ad seemed to be about the Black Lives Matter (BLM) movement, the casting of Jenner seemed misguided. The ad dispute brought Pepsi's purchase consideration score and brand perception among millennials down from 27 per cent to 24 per cent from early April to mid-July. After November, purchase consideration was down to 23 per cent, the lowest since April 2015. A year after pulling out its controversial Kendall Jenner ad, Pepsi's millennial brand perception remained low. It led to the lowest level of purchase consideration in three years.

After the incident, PepsiCo had pulled the advertisement out off the air and the Internet in less than forty-eight hours. PepsiCo also published a short press release on their website and Twitter:

> *Pepsi was trying to bring forward a global message of unity, peace, and understanding. We obviously missed the mark, and we apologise for that. We did not intend to shed light on any serious matter. We are removing the content and halting any further roll-out. We also apologise to put Kendall Jenner in this position.*

In summary, Pepsi had maintained an impressive social media channel that worked to provide customer experience, drive high user engagement, and create a higher level of customer loyalty. A social media advertisement campaign was essential to a business strategy that could shape customer perception and attitudes towards PepsiCo and influence purchase decisions. Most of Pepsi's video campaigns had become so successful that they could leverage the power of social media channels. Moreover, leveraging these social media channels could keep fans and followers updated.

**Lessons from PepsiCo:**

- *Be sensitive to the issues of culture, politics, and human rights.* Never shed light on the political or human rights issues for the sake of a short commercial. The company needs to think about its implications to societies. Many advertisement campaigns have failed because they take advantage of critical social issues or politically-charged news events. Do not merely engage in an advertising campaign without proper research.

- *Research the potential and relevance of celebrity endorsers.* Do not just hire a celebrity endorser without considering its relevance to a specific context. This is to ensure that every campaign is effective. The selection of appropriate celebrity endorsers is based on trustworthiness, popularity, physical attractiveness, likability, and personality. Celebrity endorsers are always with public figures, community groups, or industry influencers. Just be aware of who is acting on behalf of your company and seek to align yourself with trustworthy partners. Choose a celebrity endorser whose values or character match the values proposition of the company or brand.

- *Understand customer experience.* Brand perception can change from day to day. It is important to monitor various patterns of interaction with customers regularly to gain a better understanding of the customer experience. The customers' buying habits, thoughts, and emotions must be closely monitored. Customer feedback and social media management tools can track brand mentions and spot problems.

**Discussion Questions:**

1. What do you understand about customer perception towards the PepsiCo campaign?
2. As a marketer, how would you suggest that PepsiCo change customers' negative perceptions towards the brand? How to improve millennials' purchase consideration in the future?
3. Do you think that Kendall Jenner is the right celebrity endorser for this campaign? Why or why not? Suggest to PepsiCo another celebrity you would use for the campaign and justify your choice.
4. Discuss the implications of the corporate apology for the controversial campaign. Do you think a corporate apology could change consumer attitudes towards PepsiCo brand?
5. Do you think that using social media as a platform for the campaign is asuccess? Discuss.

# CASE STUDY 10: TROPICANA

## SIMPLER BUT FAILED PACKAGING

Tropicana is one of the world's leading brands of refrigerated orange juice. It was founded by Anthony T. Rossi in 1947 in his mission to bring the best of orange juice to everyone all year round. A few years later, Tropicana engineers developed a process of flash pasteurisation to preserve the colour and flavour for fresh juice. In 1998, PepsiCo bought Tropicana from the Canadian company Seagram to compete with Coca-Cola's Minute Maid product in the fresh juice market.

PepsiCo had long packaged Tropicana Pure Premium orange juice in coated-paper cartons that featured a big juicy orange with a straw sticking out of it. It was designed to send the message that Tropicana brand orange juice is very fresh. The packaging was eye-catching and created strong appeal on the store shelf.

PepsiCo hired an advertisement agency for US$35 million to modernise the packaging for its flagship products. The company wanted to introduce a simpler and updated look for its Tropicana

Pure Premium orange juice brand. The major package redesign was launched in early 2009. In the new package design, the classic straw-in-orange symbol was replaced by a glass filled with coloured orange juice. The words '100% orange pure and natural' were prominently displayed on the new packaging to remind the consumers about the health benefits of the juice. Tropicana president Neil Campbell was quoted saying, 'We wanted to create an emotional attachment by "heroing" the juice and trumpeting the natural fruit goodness'.

Consumers swiftly rejected the packaging changes. The newly-launched packaging was described as 'ugly', 'stupid', and resembling 'a generic bargain brand' on social media. Consumers claimed they had difficulty to differentiate between the company's orange juice and other juice varieties. They also complained about taking longer time to find the products on the shelves.

Over the first two months, sales of Tropicana Pure Premium orange juice declined by 20 per cent or roughly US$33 million. The president acknowledged it had been a mistake and the management had 'underestimated the deep emotional bond' consumers had with the original packaging. Merely after six weeks, PepsiCo scraped the new packaging and announced that it would bring back the previous design.

**Lessons from Tropicana:**

- *Ask your customers about your brand.* Do proper marketing research before making major changes in your iconic design as it may harm your brand visibility.
- *Leverage on your brand.* Do not underestimate the emotional attachment of your customers to the classic packaging. Product identification and recognition should not be overly modified while modernising the brand.
- *Be careful and be patient.* Explain to your consumers why a change needed to be made so customers know what to expect and can be prepared.
- *Listen, listen, listen.* If your customers completely rejected the new packaging or the sales went down, switch back to the old, familiar design.

**Discussion Questions:**

1. PepsiCo scrapped the new packaging and reverted to the old straw-stuck-in-an-orange version after rapid drop in sales and thousands of complaints. Do you agree or disagree about the decision made by PepsiCo? Why?
2. Assess PepsiCo's efforts to manage brand equity for its flagship product, Tropicana Pure Premium orange juice, in the last five years. What actions has it taken to be innovative and relevant? Can you suggest any changes to its marketing programme?
3. PepsiCo advertised its Tropicana Pure Premium orange juice with the words '100% pure and natural' on the packaging. In your opinion, how do this health claim influence consumers' evaluations of this product?

# PART II

## APPAREL, BEAUTY PRODUCTS, AND FOOTWEAR

Adidas
Dolce & Gabbana
Dove
Gap
H&M
JCPenney

# CASE STUDY 11: ADIDAS

## ABUSE OF TWITTER PERSONALISATION

Adidas AG is founded and headquartered in Herzogenaurach, Germany, by Adolf Dassler. He was joined by his elder brother Rudolf in 1924 under the name Dassler Brothers Shoe Factory. Dassler assisted in the development of spiked running shoes (spikes) for multiple athletic events. The company focused on the design and manufacture of shoes, clothing, and accessories. It was the largest sportswear manufacturer in Europe and the second largest in the world, after Nike.

The company aims to make the best sports products and to satisfy consumers in the best way possible. Their current strategic business model was called Creating the New. The emphasis of this model was on how brands interacted and communicated with consumers. However, to fulfil the current model, the brand had often concentrated on building a culture of performance. Adidas's latest strategy approach was based on three strategic choices: 'SPEED' – How We Deliver, 'CITIES' – Where We Deliver and 'OPEN SOURCE' – How We Create.

Through its origins in the sports industry, Adidas contends that sport plays a vital role in the lives of more and more people. Sports is fundamental to every culture and society. It is essential for people's health and enjoyment. As such, Adidas aims to encourage and empower people to make the most of sport in their lives. Therefore, Adidas has always sought to expand its existing products, experiences, and services to drive brand desire and grow in sport-inspired casual and athletic apparel. Adidas focuses on the development of inspirational and creative content concepts that stimulate customer advocacy as well as brand value. Adidas utilises its marketing activities to build trust between its customers for achieving this goal. One of Adidas's marketing strategies to reinforce its brand is to leverage its secondary association with the Arsenal Football Club to strengthen its brand equity.

Adidas has launched a 2019/20 home kit to kick off a brand-new partnership between Adidas and Arsenal, which aims to raise the club both on and off the field. Adidas explained on the collaboration with Arsenal, 'Arsenal has always had a unique culture that has seen them at the forefront of innovation, redefining the game, while remaining true to their core values'. While Arsenal stated that 'Adidas's core values reflect ours, they are progressive and innovative, and their bold ambitions for the club and the partnership are aligned with our own'.

In July 2019, Adidas UK unveiled a social media campaign to promote its new jerseys for the Arsenal English Premier League club. The advertisement campaign allowed users to have their Twitter handle generated by sharing or like a promotional tweet on the back of the new jerseys. The images were accompanied by a link inviting users to purchase personalised shirts. Adidas UK then shared the personalised photos to their 832,000 followers and tweeted from the @adidasUK account. Anyone who used the hashtag #DareToCreate would automatically receive a reply from Adidas UK's Twitter account on the back of the Arsenal shirt. However, images of Arsenal kits referring to Adolf Hitler, Madeleine McCann, and the Hillsborough were subsequently shared when Twitter users realised that the artificial intelligence tool did not filter out offensive usernames.

The campaign was centred on the hashtag #DareToCreate. Anyone who tweeted the hashtag or liked the company's promotional tweets would receive an automatically-generated reply featuring a picture of an Arsenal jersey with the user's Twitter handled emblazoned on the back, along with a link to purchase one of the jerseys.

The official @adidasUK account also retweeted those images to its 832,000 followers on Monday and Tuesday, which was when people began to notice Arsenal jerseys with Twitter handles such as @GasAllJewss, @DieAllN****rs, @InnocentHitler, and @96wasnotenough. People with those accounts referred to tragic incidents, such as the Hillsborough disaster, the worst in British sporting history when ninety-six people were crushed while watching the FA Cup marched inside a stadium in 1989, and the disappearance of British child Madeleine McCann in 2007.

The controversial issue arose when some users changed their handles to offensive phrases such as @GasAllJews and @InnocentHitler, which led Adidas UK to tweet messages like '@GasAllJews This is home. Welcome to the squad'. Twitter account handle backfired. Adidas used artificial intelligence (AI) to respond to users. However, it was wrong when Twitter users with offensive handle caught on, leading to images of the Arsenal jerseys with racist and insensitive messages on their backs.

Following the incident, Adidas responded by immediately switching off the functionality and asking Twitter to investigate the incident. Arsenal was aware of the Twitter personalisation mechanic designed to allow excited fans to get their name on the back of the new jersey had been abused. The tweets had since been removed, and both Adidas and Arsenal apologised. Twitter, as an innovative provider, had identified an investigation that the racist social media users had abused the account. Also, it was found that the social media account automatically-generated reply messages to users using artificial intelligence; however, the bots went wrong.

**Lessons from Adidas:**

- ***Have a tool to track the remarks, comments, and statuses on social media.*** Tools such as Brandwatch and Social Mention allow you to monitor your online reputation. Some tools will send you notifications when specific comments associated with your company are made on social media.
- ***Do the right thing.*** If your advertisement missed the mark, own the mistake and do not get defensive. Always deliver a heartfelt apology that offers the same message across every channel and audience.
- ***Create successful social media content.*** Use social media to connect with your audience and showcase your brand's personality. Take advantage of all available social media platforms to promote relationships with customers. Try to grab users' attention by creating a catchy headline, image, video, or memes.

**Discussion Questions:**

1. Evaluate Adidas's response towards the incident in the case. What else can be done?
2. What are the advantages and disadvantages of leveraging secondary brand association through partnership?
3. As a marketing consultant, propose several ways to generate business and grow your brand by using social media.
4. If you are on Adidas management, how would you suggest to your teams to optimise social media marketing strategy?

# CASE STUDY 12: DOLCE & GABBANA

## 'DEAD & GONE' IN CHINA

The Italian luxury fashion house Dolce & Gabbana was established by Domenico Dolce and Stefano Gabbana. Started in 1985, the brand made a huge debut on the international fashion scene. In 2018, Dolce & Gabbana was excited to have its first-ever fashion show in China. It was scheduled to be held on 21 November in Shanghai. Four days before the show, the luxury brand launched a series of promotional videos on Weibo, the Chinese social media network, to promote the brand's biggest show ever. And the campaign was called #DGTheGreatShow.

The promotional videos with the tag #DGLovesChina featured a young Chinese model in a sequin red dress attempting to eat Italian dishes with a pair of chopsticks. In the first video, a Mandarin-speaking voiceover kicked in: 'Welcome to episode 1 with Dolce & Gabbana's *Eating with Chopsticks*. First up today is how to use this stick-shaped cutlery to eat your *great* traditional pizza margherita'. The second and third videos showed the same model was struggling to tackle pasta and cannoli with chopsticks while making funny facial expressions.

The campaign was meant to be funny. But the company got it wrong and provoked public outrage. The videos were perceived as culturally insensitive, racist, disrespectful, and promoting unflattering stereotypes. In less than twenty-four hours, the company removed the videos.

The controversy escalated further when a Chinese fashion blogger shared a screenshot of private conversation between the company's co-founder Stefano Gabbana and an Instagram user. In the chat, Gabbana appeared to make racist comments about the Chinese people. However, the company claimed its Instagram and Gabbana's accounts had been hacked, and both founders apologised for the posts. The message went viral, and many Chinese people considered the apology as insincere.

Many agencies decided to pull their models out of the show, and a number of influencers cancelled their appearances in protest of the brand's show. The designers had to cancel the show a few hours before it was scheduled to take place. It lost around €20 million that had been spent in preparation for the mega fashion show. Since then, Chinese e-commerce sites began pulling out Dolce & Gabbana's products from their websites. Celebrities and consumers in China also called for a boycott of the brand.

**Lessons from Dolce & Gabbana:**

- *Be sensitive to cultural differences.* When dealing with unfamiliar markets, it is important to understand local cultures and values. Carefully study the local market and its intricacies.
- *Be 'politically correct'.* Hire a local team when making decisions. A new marketing campaign should be sincere, authentic, and culturally appropriate.
- *Be vigilant.* React immediately and address each negative comment before it escalates into bigger issue.
- *Be sincere in your apology.* Do not be afraid to apologise when a crisis happens. It is better to be responsible than to find excuses for a mistake.
- *Brand-equity building is critical.* The power of social media can be a double-edged sword for marketing. Use it wisely to create value to your brand.

**Discussion Questions:**

1. Assess Dolce & Gabbana's efforts to manage brand equity in the last five years. What actions has it taken to be relevant in China and other markets? Can you suggest any changes to Dolce & Gabbana's marketing programme?
2. How Dolce & Gabbana can regain the trust from customers in China after advertisement backlash?
3. Evaluate Dolce & Gabbana's response in the crisis. What did they do well? What did they not do well?

# CASE STUDY 13: DOVE

## RACISM IN ADVERTISING

Dove is the world's leading cleansing brand. The brand is owned by a Dutch-British fast-moving consumer goods (FMCG) company Unilever. Dove offers a wide range of products, including soap, body wash, lotion, shampoo, conditioner, deodorants, etc.

In 2004, Dove launched 'Campaign for Real Beauty' in United States. The campaign was conceived after its global market research revealed that only 2 per cent of women think they are beautiful. Dove believes that beauty is for everyone and, therefore, features not skinny and beautiful models but 'real women' in the campaign.

From billboards to television commercials and YouTube videos, a unifying theme of celebrating women of all ages and sizes is used in the campaign. It makes women feel good about themselves through the inclusion of more realistic and diverse models. Over the years, the campaign has won multiple prestigious awards and gained immense popularity worldwide.

As a part of a campaign for Dove body wash, a three-second video clip was posted to the US Facebook page in October 2017. In the video, a black woman removes her brown shirt and then transforms into a light-skinned woman in a light shirt. The video hoped to convey that Dove body wash is for every woman, regardless of their skin colour. The advertisement said, 'Ready for a Dove shower? Sulphate free with 100 per cent gentle cleansers, our body wash gets top marks from dermatologists'.

The advertisement ignited firestorm of protest on social media. Many consumers felt offended and said the advertisement was 'racist' and this mistake had happened before. Twitter user Toya M. Jones said, 'Don't buy Dove soap, shower gel or lotion. Perhaps if we #BoycottDove and all Unilever products they will learn to RESPECT #blackwomen'.

Unilever quickly responded by issuing an apology and said they deeply regretted any offence caused. The company admitted it had 'missed the mark in representing women of colour thoughtfully'. The post was removed by Unilever within hours. However, the damage was done. Many social media users were angry and called for a boycott under the hashtag #DonewithDove.

**Lessons from Dove:**

- *Be sensitive.* Send a clear message to your staff and community that you support diversity and would not condone racism. Avoid producing advertisements that imply racism.
- *Communicate.* Spend time talking to your diverse audiences before releasing any advertisement on social media. Get honest feedback to avoid oversights and act on it prior publishing it to the public.

- *Have a diversified team.* Get people with diverse backgrounds, experiences, and ways of thinking to assess new marketing initiatives. Make sure they are able to speak up and share their thoughts and ideas to produce products, services, and campaigns that hit the mark.
- *Learn from your past mistake and competitors.* Examine what has worked and what has not worked for you and your competitors. Avoid making the same marketing mistakes in the future.

**Discussion Questions:**

1. Unilever found a very profitable way to market its Dove brand to women. Do you think advertising can really work to rebuild women's self-esteem and redefining beauty standards? Explain your answer.
2. Several big brands like Dove have been labelled 'racist' after releasing advertisement on social media. Why they keep making the same mistake? Has racism become a marketing tool for brands?
3. In 2020, the Dove brand was valued at approximately US$4.97 billion. Assess Unilever's recent efforts to manage Dove's brand equity.

# CASE STUDY 14: GAP

## THE SHORT-LIVED LOGO

The Gap Inc., or commonly known as Gap, is the world's well-known American clothing, accessories, and personal care products retailer. The company's brands include Old Navy, Gap, Banana Republic, Athleta, Intermix, Janie and Jack, and Hill City brands. The first Gap store was founded in 1969 by Don Fisher and his wife Doris in San Francisco. Don named the store as The Gap to refer to generation gap (the differences between the boomers and the silent generation).

On 4 October 2010, the apparel chain unveiled a new company logo to rejuvenate its brand image. It was the first redesign of its logo after more than twenty years. Gap's old logo consists of white serif capitals on a dark blue square. The new logo had the word 'Gap' written in lowercase, black Helvetica font with a small blue square over the letter 'p'.

A spokeswoman for San Francisco-based Gap, Louise Callagy, believed the old logo was old and *tired*. She said, 'It was a natural fit to see how the logo, the one that we've had for over twenty years, should evolve and since our brands and our clothes are changing, we want a new logo to reflect that change'. The makeover signalled the company is changing. Unfortunately, Gap's logo redesign was met with tremendous consumer backlash. Within hours after the logo release, customers took to Twitter to voice their dismay (e.g., "This is the worst idea Gap has ever had. I will be sad to see this change take place', 'Your new logo makes your brand look cheap and unappealing. It's just ugly'.).

Because of overwhelming online fury and negative consumer response, Gap capitulated on it. The company asked consumers on its Facebook page for better ideas and share their designs. This crowdsourcing initiative drew further online ire, and Gap decided not to use a new logo after all. The company announced it was retaining its twenty-year-old blue-box logo, and its management admitted missing the opportunity to engage with its customers first.

**Lessons from Gap:**

- *Change is never easy.* Changing a well-received or even iconic brand element, like a logo, always comes with risks. It is a gamble. Even if the logo looks 'old', a new logo is not always the solution for better business outcomes. Your loyal customers may react negatively towards new logo because of its unfamiliarity.
- *Communicate, communicate, communicate.* Have dialogues with your customers to co-create brand logo values. Never be afraid to ask them for their opinions about your logo change. Explain the rationale of your logo makeover and handle negative reaction carefully and patiently.

- ***Do not underestimate the customers' sense of design.*** The new logo must look professional and meet the expectations of customers. Make your logo simple and relevant. A well-designed logo can result in better market behaviour, such as increased market shares and improved financial performance.
- ***Be mindful of the potential impact.*** Changes are hard for consumers. Those who are most attached to the brand may be most sensitive to logo change. Acknowledge the potential discomfort that high-attachment consumers may have about a redesigned logo by communicating empathically with them. Show you care about how your consumer feel and value their feedbacks.

**Discussion Questions:**

1. Gap quickly returned to its iconic blue and white logo when its new logo courted online backlash. Do you think it was a good move? Would you take a different approach? Explain your answer.
2. Consumer resistance is a common response to logo change. What can managers do to successfully introduce logo redesigns?
3. Assess Gap's efforts to manage brand equity in the last five years. What actions has the American cloth retailer taken to be innovative and relevant?

# CASE STUDY 15: H&M

## CONSUMER BOYCOTT

H&M (Hennes & Mauritz) is a multinational Swedish apparel retailer founded in 1947 by Erling Persson. The first shop opened in Västerås, Sweden, was known as Hennes (Swedish for 'hers'); the exclusive women's clothing store opened in Norway in 1964. Four years later, in 1968, Persson collaborated with the apparel retailer Mauritz Widforss to expand the market by including the men's clothing collection. With a combination of names, Persson changed the stores to Hennes & Mauritz. As of 2019, H&M operates in seventy-four countries with over five thousand stores under different company brands, including both physical and online stores. H&M also utilised webshops through modern technology, digital innovation, and social media platforms to enhance customer's seamless shopping experience.

The promotion of H&M marketing varies. However, one of the advertisements posted on the website and the social media platforms received considerable criticism in January 2018. H&M UK caused a global uproar by advertising a green hoodie with the slogan 'Coolest

Monkey in the Jungle' in its online store featuring a black boy model, while a white child model wore an orange sweatshirt saying 'Mangrove Jungle' on the front.

Immediately, the company was confronted with an outcry on social media from celebrities, journalists, advocates of social justice, and consumers, most of whom widely criticised advertising as racist, offensive, degrading, and negligent. Furthermore, the company was criticised for showing a severe lack of social awareness and racial sensitivity (cf. Bever 2018).

There were many consequences after the incident. Among them was the hashtag #BoycottHM appeared on Twitter, expressing their criticism and joining the protest against the clothing giant. Several parties announced the end of collaboration include The Weeknd (Canadian pop star) announced the end of his collaboration with H&M and deleted pictures of his two H&M clothing collections. NBA star, LeBron James, known for speaking up about social issues, shared an altered image with a crowned child. He said, 'I see a young King!' (The King James, 2018).

Several stores of the Swedish brand had been closed down and vandalised by activists and protesters in South Africa. In the closure of all H&M stores in South Africa, the police had to intervene to stop the violence and to ensure the safety of staff and customers. Furthermore, public criticism also led to a decline in H&M's shares on the stock market. They had dropped to their lowest level since April 2009. This was a further setback since the company had already reported a decline in sales in December 2017 and announced the closure of the stores. However, there was some feedback from Twitter users who supported the H&M ad as a lack of cultural awareness and racial sensitivity and thought that the advertisement was cute.

H&M apologised for an image on its UK online store featuring a black child in a green hoodie, with the phrase 'Coolest Monkey in the Jungle' printed on the hoodie. The apology arose after the Swedish retailer had copped the flak for a loaded term, as the monkey was often used in racial and ethnic slurs, especially against the black community. Meanwhile, H&M also engaged a white child to model two other versions of the garment, one of which featured the phrase 'Mangrove Jungle Survival Expert' while the other showcased jungle animal prints. In their statement, 'We sincerely apologise for offending people with this image of a printed hooded top. The image has been removed from all online channels and the product will not be for sale in the United States, We believe in diversity and inclusion in all that we do and will review all our internal policies accordingly to avoid any future issues'.

H&M had honestly admitted their mistake and deeply regretted the photo taken. The company explained that it was their fault that routines and process were not adequately monitored. H&M promised to investigate the cases thoroughly and to avoid similar mistakes in the future. As a result of this incident, H&M removed the image of the black child from its channels and the green hoodie from its global product offering. Still, the product would be available in the UK market.

There were many arguments about the advertisement of a hoodie featured in the black child model. The company should be more sensitive to global culture. The use of a monkey was historically perceived as inappropriate because it was racially and ethnically decried. Comparing the black people to a monkey meant a racist undertone because of its historical use to demean and dehumanise people of African descent.

**Lessons from H&M:**

- *An honest and timely response can turn a situation around.* It is not easy to admit that you were wrong and ask for forgiveness. Effective corporate apologies can fix a public relation disaster. Instead of running away, outline what your company did wrong, take responsibility, and issue a genuine apology. Do not be defensive or make excuses. A heartfelt apology will resonate with consumers and help mend the trust that was broken. Besides, assure your customers that you have learned from the experience and the mistake will not happen again.
- *Always be sensitive.* A truly effective diversity campaign always begins with understanding your customers and your marketplace. Learn about their culture and ways of doing business. Also, develop policies, procedures, and handbooks that comply with local laws while maintaining balance with overall company policies.
- *Listen to your customers.* Companies that invest in customer experience see financial gains. You should build a company culture where every team thinks customer first and takes customer experience as a collective responsibility.
- *Diverse marketing teams.* Marketing teams with a diverse mix of members tend to produce better results. You need to have a variety of voices in your team to avoid culturally insensitive missteps.

**Discussion Questions:**

1. Define culture. Distinguish beliefs, values, and customs from one another. Explain how the children's clothing in the advertisement has influenced consumer purchasing decisions?
2. Do you think that H&M's tagline is a rational one? Why or why not? Do you believe that the actions taken by H&M are acceptable?
3. How would you suggest an effective marketing campaign strategy targeted at children globally?
4. Find two different apparel brand advertisements on other social media platforms that target children. Analyse its content and visual aspects of each advertisement. What are the core values communicated through their advertisements? How are these values portrayed to target audience?

# CASE STUDY 16: JCPENNEY

## 'FAIR AND SQUARE' PRICING?

J. C. Penney Company (JCPenney), Inc. is founded by James Cash Penney in 1902. Today the major retailer sells various merchandise and services to consumers through its 846 department stores and their website at jcp.com in the United States. JCPenney primarily sell apparel, handbags, footwear, accessories, jewellery, home furnishings, and beauty products. The company also provides a variety of in-store services, such as styling salon, optical, and portrait photography.

A former retail chief at Apple, Ron Johnson, was appointed as the new CEO of JCPenney in November 2011. Johnson initiated a turnaround plan to elevate the company's brand image in February 2012. In an attempt to simplify prices at JCPenney, Johnson introduced a new pricing strategy that completely eliminates annual sale events. At the same time, all prices ended in '0' instead of '99,' and price tags were listed with just one price. He dubbed the campaign as 'Fair and Square'—a simple, transparent way for customers to buy.

Shoppers were not happy with the changes made by Johnson. They were accustomed to hunt for deals by using cash coupons and price markdowns. JCPenney's customers felt there is no sense of urgency to buy at JCPenney and left to shop elsewhere. Throughout 2012, JCPenney's sales and market share continued to plummet.

Only after a few months, Johnson admitted he was wrong and went too fast with the changes. JCPenney returned to coupons and weekly advertised sales. After seventeen months on the job as CEO, Johnson lost his job. He was replaced by his predecessor, Mike Ullman.

**Lessons from JCPenney:**

- *Engage with your customers.* Connect well with your customers to understand their needs, views, and insights.
- *Do appropriate research.* Before making any shift in your existing plan, do a survey or get feedback from your customers. Your new plans may result in unintended consequences.
- *What works for one brand might not work for another.* High-end brands with more unique merchandise may be able to operate with fewer sales and promotions. If you sell commodity-like products, everyday pricing strategies may not work well.
- *Give a reason for your customers to shop at your store.* If your existing customers love sales and expect sales events, do not try eliminate those sales events.
- *Take time to make a change.* Even you have good intentions, it is not good enough. Ease customers into changes you plan to make.

**Discussion Questions:**

1. Would you suggest to JCPenney to reveal the marked up or original prices for all merchandise at JCPenney as a way to prove that its everyday prices are really low?
2. JCPenney failed to rebrand its stores with a new 'fair and square' pricing strategy. Shoppers were confused and disappointed. Why do you think this strategy did not work for shoppers at JCPenney?
3. Do you think JCPenney still have a place in today's retail world? How the stores be revitalised and create some excitement to engage customers?

# PART III

## AUTOMOBILE, BANKING SERVICES, AND MOBILE TECHNOLOGY

BMW
HSBC
Samsung Galaxy Fold
Samsung Galaxy Note 7

# CASE STUDY 17: BMW

## COMMERCIAL FEATURING UAE ANTHEM

The luxury automobile maker BMW (Bayerische Motoren Werke AG) is based in Munich, Germany. The company posted a sales record of 2.5 million of BMW, MINI, and Rolls-Royce vehicles in 2019. The company has garnered huge amount publicity for having its cars featured in James Bond films. BMW was ranked thirty-second in *Fortune Magazine*'s list of the 2020 World's Most Admired Companies.

In 2016, BMW's distributors in United Arab Emirates has pulled a television commercial after local citizens complained on social media about the use of the country's national anthem in a television advertisement. The thirty-second advertisement was first aired on 31 May 2016. It showed Al Ain football players singing "Ishy Biladi" ("Long Live My Country") before a match in a packed stadium. Halfway through, they stopped singing and rushed out of the stadium after hearing the car engines revving outside the stadium. At the end of the advertisement, the players proudly drove off the latest models of luxury BMW cars.

The advertisement aimed to show the football players' desire and passion for BMW cars. However, it has drawn a public outcry over social media sites. A hashtag 'stop BMW ads' in Arabic language was among the top trending topics on Twitter after the advertisement was aired. Viewers found the advertisement was inappropriate as the football players behaved in a disrespectful manner when the song is played in the advertisement.

BMW and Abu Dhabi Motors quickly responded by pulling the advertisement in response to the backlash. BMW said they intended to show players running towards the cars after the national anthem ended, but the advertisement had to be cut off because of time restriction for the video.

In a press statement, the general manager for Abu Dhabi Motors said, 'We have noted the recent concerns regarding our TV Commercial with the Al Ain Football Club. As proud and loyal members of the UAE community, it was never our intention to cause any offence. We are an Emirati-owned company and so always aim to celebrate and promote the UAE's rich values and culture, which are rightfully recognised around the world for excellence across all aspects of daily life'.

**Lessons from BMW:**

- ***Show respect to national anthem.*** When featuring a national anthem in any advertisement or marketing campaign, make sure you use it properly and with due respect. Make sure the advertisement follows the standard and etiquette when the national anthem is played or sung.

- **Be ready and well prepared.** Sending the wrong message to your audience will spark controversy and lead to a customer backlash. Make sure you always send the right one!
- **Look before you leap.** Get your appropriate employees to review your advertising and get their approval. Furthermore, test your advertisement by showing it to existing customers and asking for feedback before you launch it to the public.
- **Build a positive image.** Make sure your advertisement is consistent with your desired business image. Anticipate how your customers will response to your advertisement.
- **Listen to your customers.** Pull out an advertisement immediately if it created a massive public outcry from multiple corners.

**Discussion Questions:**

1. A national anthem is the symbol and sign of a nation. It was quite surprising when BMW made a huge mistake of improperly using the UAE national anthem in a television commercial. What can marketers do if they want to feature models singing the national anthem in their advertisements?
2. Why global companies like BMW must get cross-cultural marketing right? How you can become successful with customers who are different from you?
3. All marketers make mistake. If your company made the same mistake like the distributors of BMW in UAE, what will you do to fix your company brand image after making the mistake?

# CASE STUDY 18: HSBC

## TOO LATE FOR 'DO NOTHING'

The Hongkong and Shanghai Banking Corporation (HSBC) Limited was founded by Thomas Sutherland in Hong Kong. HSBC opened its doors in 1865. HSBC took over UK-based Midland Bank in 1992 and established HSBC Holdings plc in London as their parent company. Today it is one of the world's leading banks and serve more than forty million customers around the world.

In 2009, the bank introduced 'Assume Nothing' campaign in the effort to enter into international markets and rebrand its global private banking operations. The campaign did well in United States for five years. Unfortunately, in some countries, the slogan 'Assume Nothing' was translated as 'Do Nothing'. Definitely, it did not work out as that was the last thing the bank wanted the customers to think what their financial managers are doing or what they want their customers to do.

HSBC quickly scraped the campaign and spent US$10 million to rebrand HSBC's private bank slogan to 'The World's Private Bank', which has a better translation into many languages.

**Lessons from HSBC:**
- *Go beyond straight translation.* Do not rely on word-to-word translation and use back translation to reduce translation errors. Make sure your intended message is actually being presented to different audiences, which speak different languages.
- *Reach out beyond your own word.* Translating advertisement text requires experience. Learn what is 'right' in other cultures. Talk to people who had experience with those in other cultures. Socialise with people from different backgrounds. Take cross-cultural course or attend cultural festivals.
- *Research, research, research.* The wording used in advertisements must be well researched to ensure that the marketing message makes sense to different target cultures. Find answers for questions, such as What do we need to convey? Who are we talking to? What are their history, values, beliefs, and practices? and How and where the target will see the message?
- *Do not rush to push a global campaign.* Use a slogan that can be translate well when you go global. Allow enough time for quality translations and engage a language provider or translation service provider to pick up translation glitches and help you communicate your brand effectively with different audiences.
- *Be ready to change.* When your company make blunders in international business through words, quickly make an effort

to fix it. A good slogan matters as it can negatively affect your company's brand image and reputation.

**Discussion Questions:**

1. A positive meaning may change to a negative one after direct translation. Suggest what global companies like HSBC can do to minimise translation errors in their worldwide marketing campaign?
2. Do you think HSBC's private bank slogan, 'The World's Private Bank', is a good slogan? Why? In your opinion, what are the characteristics of a good marketing slogan?
3. In 2019, HSBC unveiled its own sound identity—'The Sound of HSBC'—and used it in their marketing campaigns worldwide. What are the advantages of using an audio branding strategy for a global company such as HSBC?

# CASE STUDY 19: SAMSUNG GALAXY FOLD

## NEW-GEN GALAXY FOLD BROKEN

The Samsung Group is a multinational South Korean conglomerate headquartered in Samsung Town, Seoul. The company was founded by Lee Byung-Chul in 1938. Samsung has diversified its business to include consumer electronics, construction, food processing, textiles, insurance, securities, and retail. Samsung has a corporate philosophy of dedicating its skills and technologies to the production of superior goods and services to support a better global community. This philosophy underlines that the goods and services offered to consumers are superior quality. At the same time, Samsung aims to deliver goods and services to ensure consumers are happy and contribute to the welfare and development of society. The view reveals innovation-intensive technologies.

In addition, Samsung has developed a reputation for showcasing creative goods that lead to social stability on cutting-edge technology such as smartphones, computers, and appliances. Samsung claims that its position in the electronics and other goods industry is a key opportunity to change people's lives and to better improve communities. Samsung shows that its focus is not just on the immediate customer who benefits from the purchase of its products.

Samsung has received several awards over the years as an innovative organisation capable of manufacturing well-designed, environmentally, and conscious goods. The prestigious Consumer Electronics Show (CES) awarded Samsung fourteen years in a row for creativity and product design. One of the main strengths of Samsung is its large range of products. Smartphones are Samsung's biggest product and still its main sales driver. The company continued to acquire new companies to broaden its product range and accelerate its growth.

The business has brought a vast spectrum of smartphones and tablets. Among other smartphones, the Samsung Galaxy line as a range of luxury phones has achieved an enormous global prominence targeting a higher-end market. Samsung's latest innovation is the Samsung Galaxy Fold. Samsung has been working on this first-gen smartphone folding products for years. Smartphone Samsung Galaxy Fold was launched in April 2019 but was released in South Korea in November 2019.

Samsung's folding phone was due to be launched in 2017, then moved back to 2018 before being delayed again to September 2019. The fact that Samsung's folding Galaxy phone has been all too quiet lately. However, since Huawei announced the launch of a folding smartphone, Samsung is also announcing to launch the fold brand. As Samsung is known as an innovator in the technology industry, it is always their aim to launch innovation and does not allow other competitors to launch innovation. This has put Samsung at risk of product failures.

The product went wrong shortly after its launch in April 2019. The Galaxy Fold reported that the displays on their units had broken after only two days of use. The company said the Galaxy Fold display was durable enough for two hundred thousand folding and unfolding. Still, some units barely lasted a couple of days. One of the reviewers commented that he removed a plastic-film display cover from the Galaxy Fold, which Samsung said would not release. It seemed that Samsung's instructions were not clear to consumers. This was because the plastic screen coating was not as premium or durable as the traditional glass smartphone screen. Critics also expressed concerns about the Galaxy Fold's susceptibility to damage by wreckage caused by the lack of protection around the display hinge, the damage to the screens of several review units in this manner, or the accidental removal of the protective plastic layer on the top of the screen (which could be mistaken as a standard screen protector).

The biggest problem appeared to be that the foldable OLED screen of the phone had a thin plastic layer on the top with exposed edges, so it looked like a screen protector. For customers, Samsung initially advised that the special protective layer that coated the screen should not be removed as this may cause damage to the screen. However, consumers might be mistaken for a pre-installed screen protector without proper warnings contained a disclaimer. Samsung later promised to do further investigation. It seems like the alerts from Samsung regarding the removal of the plastic film could not have been explicit enough.

After the incident, Samsung called all the broken phone and began investigating potential causes of various failures. The company might have already shared an updated release date with the partners. If it were true, Samsung put the cart ahead of the horse, and customers would have little or no confidence that the company was doing everything in its power to fix the phone's problems ahead of release. Because of this incident, Samsung had to stop production and take a break. Furthermore, Samsung had postponed the Chinese launch event; Samsung announced on 22 April that the launch (initially scheduled for 26 April) had been delayed because they were working to fix the issue, with plans to announce the release date sometime in the coming weeks. Samsung later announced that Galaxy Fold's pre-orders would automatically be cancelled if the device had not been shipped by 31 May. The customers had not otherwise confirmed their orders. In response to these issues, Samsung announced that it would delay the release of the Galaxy Fold indefinitely while addressing the problems.

**Lessons from Samsung Galaxy Fold:**

- ***Conduct sound research for the systematic development of new products.*** It takes a long process to launch a new product.
- ***Consumers are sceptical about new products on the market.*** Building and restoring consumer confidence are essential. Employing advertising and promotion, the company needs to develop marketing strategies to build consumer confidence, in particular in new products and failed products of the same brand.
- ***Manage customer perception and communicate multiple channels of communication clearly to customers.*** Seek an apology for the incident and promise to do the investigation

to compensate customers for the failure. Provide better customer service to improve corporate reputation and brand image.

- ***Be innovative and creative to create a differentiation.*** Consumers always change their desires and preferences. The best value that can be offered at a reasonable price can change the consumer's mindset. To be different, the company should study the strategies of its competitors, be innovative, and understand consumer needs, wants, values, trends, and preferences.
- ***Have strategic pricing.*** Price is always linked to quality. Customers still have high expectations of high prices. The company needs to ensure that it delivers the brand values correctly, i.e. high-quality products, if the price is set at a premium to win consumer trust and confidence. Identify the products and categories of products that make up most of your sales and price them competitively while keeping other prices high.

**Discussion Questions:**

1. Explain the brand positioning of the Samsung Galaxy Fold. What is the possible customer perception of the Samsung brand when this incident occurs?
2. What are the success factors in the adoption of innovative technology? What are the resistance factors for the adoption of technology? Discuss the type of group adopters.
3. What is stage of the product lifecycle is this Samsung Galaxy Fold? Discuss. Describe which marketing strategies are appropriate for this stage.

4. You are the product manager of an electrical company. Propose a new product category and discuss how to implement a new systematic process of product development. What are the critical considerations to launch a successful new product?

# CASE STUDY 20: SAMSUNG GALAXY NOTE 7

## SMARTPHONE EXPLODES

Samsung is the largest chaebol (family-run conglomerate) in South Korea. It was a small trading company founded by Lee Byung-Chul in 1938. Samsung means three stars. The stars are the three wishes of the founder: to grow the company bigger, stronger, and forever. His wishes came true, and today Samsung is one of the world's largest manufacturer of consumer electronics, semiconductors, and mobile phones.

Samsung Galaxy Note series is a series of high-end Android smartphones with large screens. The series are developed and marketed by Samsung Electronics since 2011. Samsung Galaxy Note 7 was officially launched on 19 August 2016, just weeks before its closest rival, Apple, was expected to release iPhone 7 and iPhone 7 Plus. The Note 7 has dual camera, a new iris scanner, and a finer point stylus ("S pen"). It is also water-resistant and can be charged wirelessly.

The Note 7 was well received by reviewers across the globe. Unfortunately, Samsung had to initiate a recall of new Note 7 in September 2016 following numerous unfortunate incidents of its faulty lithium-ion battery. There were multiple reports of the device either igniting or exploding.

Initially, Samsung offered to exchange the recalled the faulty phones with new units of Note 7s. The replacement units were powered by safer battery sourced from a different supplier. However, Samsung yet again faced reports of batteries overheating and phones bursting into flames.

By 7 October 2016, Samsung officially stopped Note 7 production completely and had to expand its recall globally. The company advised users to stop using the device. They were given a choice of either getting a full refund or change to another Samsung phone. Samsung even set up Note 7 trade-in booths at major airports around the world as some major airlines banned the device. Samsung said it lost about US$5 billion caused by this crisis.

Samsung wrote an open letter of apology to all Galaxy Note7 customers. Besides, Samsung published a full-page advert in multiple U.S. newspapers to apologise for falling short on the company's ambition to 'offer best-in-class safety and quality'. In 2017, Samsung announced the results of their investigations on Note 7 and concluded that the batteries were found to be the cause of the Note 7 incidents. The company admitted their failure to identify the issues arising out of the battery design and manufacturing process prior to the launch of the Note 7. The company promised the problem would not recur.

**Lessons from Samsung Galaxy Note 7:**

- *Handle recall properly.* Apologise and take action quickly. Handle massive product recall with care as it will determine your company's future success or failure. Ensure your products is safely returned and compensate your customers in fast and fairly manner.
- *Be as open and transparent.* If there is a problem with your product, initiate an investigation to analyse what went wrong and share the results with the public. Explain the problem to your customers and prevent something similar from happening in the future.
- *Test rigorously.* Every product should be subjected to rigorous testing. Assess every step of manufacturing process and develop safety checks for your products.

**Discussion Questions:**

1. What crisis did Samsung's marketing team face during the recall of Samsung Galaxy Note 7? How well did they handle the recall?
2. What alternative recall strategies would you advised Samsung to consider and how should the company implement the strategies?
3. Identify Samsung's sources of brand equity. Assess its level of brand awareness and the strength, favourability, and uniqueness of its associations.

# KEY TAKEAWAYS

Marketing is the heart of your business. Business success comes with clear objectives, unique values proposition, mission, and vision statement. Successful businesses are built over years. It requires careful planning and the ability to manage resources effectively. Therefore, managers must have effective business planning skills to handle people and businesses. For those who are thinking about starting a new business, they should begin with defining the marketing concept. Do a quick search for existing companies in your chosen industry. Explore and learn what current business are doing. Find out how you can do it better than them. You may think of your business can deliver something other companies don't or deliver the same thing but offer better values for example faster and cheaper. Dare to be different from other competitors. When you have something that can help consumers to solve their problem then, you've got a solid idea and are ready to create a business plan. Then do market research.

On the other hand, for those already in the business, keep learning how to grow and sustain your business for a long-term. Business strategies are dynamic; Thus, never give up and feel complacent about your business position in the marketplace. You always need to keep yourselves abreast with the micro and macro marketing environmental changes.

Let's understand the meaning of *marketing*. Marketing is one of the business functions that deal with external stakeholders, particularly customers. The primary aim of a business to attract and retain its customers. Therefore, always make sure your current customers are happy and make repeat purchases. Make them feel valued and reward those who are loyal to your brand.

Most of the time, customers are aware of their needs, preference, and wants. However, sometimes, they are not. Thus, as a marketer, you need to create customer awareness, and make them recognise the problems of not using your products. Next, you need to design specific marketing strategies for your target market segments, and decide on value propositions. At this stage, branding plays a critical role to create a product differentiation.

Subsequently, design marketing programs to communicate and deliver your value offerings or brand promise to potential customers. At this stage, you need to be creative and selective in choosing the right marketing channels. Capitalise on both traditional and digital marketing, particularly different marketing channels and social media platforms. A key formula is to tailor your communications as much as possible.

Finally, develop strategies in managing and maintaining good relationships with customers. Managers need make customer retention a priority. A satisfied customer may not be loyal; however, a committed customer tends to be loyal to your brand. Focus your marketing efforts to engage and build long-lasting relationships with customers. Show them they matter.

Managing an effective marketing strategy is very challenging. Therefore, recognising and avoiding common blunders would help business to achieve its short and long-term goals. Besides, managers must understand various business risks and develop a crisis management plan.

Business risks can be divided into strategic risk, compliance risk, operational risk, and reputational risk. Strategic risk arises when an organization is not able to react to the market conditions and needs in time. Compliance risk involves an industry or business that is highly regulated. Incompliance with certain regulations will negatively affect business.

Operational risk arises within the corporation, especially when the day-to-day operations of a company fail to perform. Lastly, reputational risk is related to a company's reputation. Through the power of social media, any kind of news (good or bad) can go viral and reach global proportions in minutes.

In sum, a crisis management plan for your business brand is an insurance policy for any unforeseen event. It shields the business's reputation and its financial value in the marketplace.

The next section summarizes the most common marketing mistakes that affect businesses.

**Common Marketing Blunders**

Marketing blunders could be derived from mistakes of designing marketing mix, branding, market segmentation, market communication, customer relationships, monitoring sales results, and marketing objectives. Some of the most common reasons for marketing blunders identified from the cases explained in this book typically fall into one or more of the following categories:

1. **Product** refers to the things or services offered to respond to customers' needs and wants in the marketplace. The product embodies benefits that provide value to customers. The mistakes include:
- Fail to understand your target market.
- Lack of unique value propositions and no real differentiation in the market.
- Failure to communicate value propositions in clear, concise and compelling fashion.
- Not really in touch with customers through deep dialogue.
- Inadequate market research.
- The products are terrible. They are designed poorly, too hard to use, lack of relative advantage, or so complex to build or maintain.

2. **Price** refers to the cost of the product and the value provided to respond to the customer needs and wants. It also refers to what customers pay. Common pricing mistakes are:
- Price is set as too high or too low. Setting prices too high might drive away customers. If setting too low, your costs may exceed the revenue generated.

- Make changes in price without understanding external factors, such as economic, demographic, and social factors. Consumers may feel frustrated and switch to your competitors.
- No clear communication on the price changes and do not give people notice well in advance about the changes.
- Customers cannot see why a direct increase in price will result in more benefits or service for them.

3. **Promotion** refers to marketing efforts you use to support the product, including messaging specific to your target market. It aims to inform, remind, and persuade customers to purchase the products. Promotion comprises mass and digital communications including advertising, sales promotion, social media, and personal communications, public relations. Some of the common promotional mistakes include:

- No specific goals to achieve. Setting clear goals helps to ensure that your marketing strategy stays on track.
- Poor or ineffective identification of the target audience.
- Inauthentic messaging. The core messaging conflicts with the actual experience customers have with the brand.
- Lack of understanding in the position stage of the product life cycle. Investment in promotional activities depends on the product life cycle. If you are in the growth stage, you may reduce the budget for promotional expenditure.
- Inappropriate use of brand elements or clues.
- Too much advertising, promotion, or sales promotion.

4. **Place or Distribution** refers to the physical and digital distribution channels that provide access to your promotional materials, marketing messaging, and enable sales. It focuses

on how and where customers could get the products. Common mistakes related to place are:
- Store cannibalisation.
- Inconsistent delivery of raw materials or supplies.
- Availability of product in stores is limited.
- Bad timing or scheduling of distribution.

5. **People** refer to staff who run a business either as front liners or back liners. Having the right people is essential for business success. Common mistakes related to people include:
- Misunderstand the target audience – their personalities, preferences, beliefs, and values.
- Poor customer service. Customer service can make or break a business. Customers want fast, helpful and friendly service.
- Fail to train the employees. Every employee must understand how important customer service is to the company, and how he or she plays a role in it.

6. **Market Segmentation** refers to a process dividing the target market into smaller and more defined that share similar characteristics based on demographics, geographical, behavioural, and psychographic. Among the common mistakes are:
- Poor or ineffective identification of the target audience.
- Fail to truly understand the needs of each consumer segment.
- Fail to determine the right market size.
- Fail to revisit your segments regularly and adjust them as needed.
- Misleading market research that does not accurately reflect the actual consumer behaviour.

**Turning Failures into Victory**

Successful marketing strategy leads to business success.

- *Be proactive.* Talk to people who are not related to your product or service about your idea and ask for advice.
- *Avoid diverting from core brand values* when launching a new product or service.
- *Update customers consistently.* Keep customers informed about fun initiatives when you offer a new product, service, or even post a new blog!
- *Use influencers.* Consider using influencers or a few well-placed spokespeople to herald the launch of a new product. It does not need to be someone famous. Someone who is respected in your community can help your business!
- *Be cautious.* A rebrand is a huge undertaking. Conduct research on your audiences, competition, and industry trends to launch a rebrand. Have a good reason for the rebrand, do not forget your core identity, and communicate to all stakeholders.
- *Time is the key!* Consider how something can be framed from all angles and prepare how to respond to these situations.
- *Craft a strong reason for the rebrand.* Making something 'modern' does not mean it will be well received. There is something to say about tradition!
- **Keep products and services** as relevant as possible and appreciated by all stakeholders.

### Recovery of Product/ Service Failures

- *Apologise.* The first step that the company needs to take is to apologise quickly and take full responsibility.
- *Analyse complaint.* The next step is to analyse the complaint to check whether there is a false claim made by customers or whether there is an absolute failure of product and service.
- *Fix the problems.* Once the company has understood the problem, tell your customers how you will make things right. Let them know how you will be better in the future and reassure them this will not happen again. Choose the best alternative and follow it up with customers.
- *Give compensation.* Show genuine remorse and compensate victims.
- *Always record the service failure.* Document the failures and provide training to improve customer service and prevent problems from recurring. Follow up to ensure that the customers will be satisfied in the future.

# CONCLUSION

Why some companies fail? What went wrong? What we can learn from the mistakes? How to create a successful marketing strategy? This book aims to answer these questions.

This goal of this book is to open up your eyes and minds to how products or businesses may have failed, even though they are still on the market. We provide cases with useful guidelines so that you can respond better to challenging market situations. Essentially, a better understanding of marketing blunders is needed to prevent future losses. Previous events provide insights into the causes of those failures and provide lessons that may increase the chances of success in the future.

This case study book is relevant and timely for students, instructors, scholars, and professionals to better understand the business marketing environment. Learn from mistakes and avoid them in the future. Moreover, you will learn how to craft good marketing campaigns.

www.ingramcontent.com/pod-product-compliance
Lightning Source LLC
Chambersburg PA
CBHW030858180526
45163CB00004B/1620